Dear Parent:
Your child's love of reading starts here!

Every child learns to read in a different way and at his or her own speed. Some go back and forth between reading levels and read favorite books again and again. Others read through each level in order. You can help your young reader improve and become more confident by encouraging his or her own interests and abilities. From books your child reads with you to the first books he or she reads alone, there are I Can Read Books for every stage of reading:

SHARED READING
Basic language, word repetition, and whimsical illustrations, ideal for sharing with your emergent reader

BEGINNING READING
Short sentences, familiar words, and simple concepts for children eager to read on their own

READING WITH HELP
Engaging stories, longer sentences, and language play for developing readers

READING ALONE
Complex plots, challenging vocabulary, and high-interest topics for the independent reader

ADVANCED READING
Short paragraphs, chapters, and exciting themes for the perfect bridge to chapter books

I Can Read Books have introduced children to the joy of reading since 1957. Featuring award-winning authors and illustrators and a fabulous cast of beloved characters, I Can Read Books set the standard for beginning readers.

A lifetime of discovery begins with the magical words "I Can Read!"

Visit www.icanread.com for information
on enriching your child's reading experience.

ISBN 978-0-06-286830-5

19 20 21 TC 10 9 8 7 6 5 4 3 2
❖
First Edition

I Can Read!

Pete the Cat's GIANT GROOVY BOOK

9 Books in One

by James Dean

HARPER

An Imprint of HarperCollinsPublishers

TABLE OF CONTENTS

Start reading with

MY FIRST!

SHARED
My
First
READING

I Can Read!

SHARED My First READING

Pete the Cat

AND THE SURPRISE TEACHER

HELLO MY NAME IS

Pete is ready for school.
"Where is Mom?" Pete asks.

"She has a surprise for you,"
says Pete's dad.

Pete goes to school.

His mom is there.

What a surprise!

"Hi, class. I am Mrs. Cat,"
says Pete's mom.
"I am the substitute teacher."

"I will need your help today,"
says Pete's mom.
"What do we do first?"

"Art!" says Pete.

"Yeah!" says the class.

The class lines up.
Pete's mom leads the line.

"Is this art?" asks Pete's mom.

Boing!

This is not art.

This is gym.

"Stay and play!"

says the gym teacher.

The class plays.
"Gym is fun with more kids!"
says Pete.

Gym is over.
Pete's mom takes
the class to art.

La, la, la!

This is not art.

This is music.
"Stay and sing!"
says the music teacher.

The class sings.
"We are louder with
more kids!" says Pete.

Rumble!

Pete is hungry.

Time for lunch!

This is not the
lunchroom.

This is the playground!
"Let's have a picnic,"
says Pete.

19

"Now it is time
for art," says Pete's mom.
Everyone cheers.

Pete leads the class.

"Is this art?"

asks Pete's mom.

It is!
Lots of kids are
making art.

"Oh no," says the art teacher.

"It is too late to join us.

The day is almost over."

The class goes to
their classroom.
"I know!" says Pete.

"Let's make art here!"

he says.

"Okay," says Pete's mom.

Pete calls a huddle.

Whisper, whisper.

The class plans a surprise.

Pete draws.

Callie makes paper cats.

Everyone helps.

"Surprise!" says Pete.
The class made art for
Pete's mom!

"Thank you, Mrs. Cat!"
says the class. "We had a
great day with you!"

Sometimes a different day

is an awesome day!

Pete the Cat

SIR PETE THE BRAVE

CAT

Meet Sir Pete,
the bravest knight
in the land!

Sir Pete rides a horse
and climbs towers.

At dinner, Sir Pete listens
to Lady Callie play the harp.
Lady Callie is awesome!

"Bravo!" Sir Pete yells
at the end of each song.
He claps louder than anyone.

One night, while Lady Callie
plays beautifully,
someone casts a spell.

And everyone falls asleep—
even Sir Pete!

The next morning,
Lady Callie is gone!
"Oh no!" says Sir Pete
the Brave.

"I will find Lady Callie
and save her."
"Giddyup!"

Sir Pete falls in a hole!
The hole is a
dragon's footprint!

"Follow the footprints!"
Sir Pete says to his horse.

41

The footprints stop!

Where did the dragon go?

Sir Pete looks up . . .

. . . and sees the dragon
flying across the lake with
Lady Callie and her harp!

Sir Pete can't fly,
but he can row.
Across the lake he goes!

Sir Pete sees a dragon cave!
He has to go inside,
but it is very dark.

Then he hears music.

He must save Lady Callie.

He won't be scared.

He finds a harp.
But no Lady Callie.

Sir Pete will not give up.

He climbs the highest hill.

He looks around for Lady

Callie.

Then he hears a loud growl.
Sir Pete is scared.

The hill starts to move!

Sir Pete is on the dragon's back!

Sir Pete knows what to do!
He slides down, down, down
the dragon's back.

The dragon sees Pete and roars!
"Sir Pete!" says Lady Callie.
"I will save you!"

"Save me?"

says Sir Pete.

"But I came to save you."

Sir Pete and Lady Callie
start to argue.
The dragon starts to cry.

55

"I just wanted to sing along."

The dragon sobs.

"I did not want to hurt anyone."

"I have an idea!" says Sir Pete.
"Will you give us a lift?"

The dragon flies Sir Pete
and Lady Callie home.
Everyone is happy to see them.

"You don't need a great
voice to make music,"
says Sir Pete. "Just good
friends!"

The dragon joins the song.
Three cheers for Lady Callie
and for Sir Pete the Brave!

Pete the Cat wakes up
and gets ready for school.
He has show-and-tell today.

"There is no school today,"
says Pete's mom.
"It's a snow day."
"Hooray!" yells Pete.

"Let's go sledding!" says Pete.
"Great idea,"
says his brother, Bob.

Pete puts on his hat,

boots, and mittens.

"I'm ready to go!" he says.

On the way,

Pete makes snowballs.

He throws one at Bob.

Bob throws one back.

Pete makes a snow cat.
"Snow days are way more fun
than school days," he says.

"Sledding hill, here we
come!" says Pete.
He can't wait to get there.

Pete waves to Callie.
"Come sledding with us,"
he says.

The hill is big.

Trey and Emma look small
at the top.

Crunch, crunch goes the snow
as Pete, Bob, and Callie
go up, up, up.

"Whee!" they yell as they go
down, down, down.

"I love snow days!"
says Pete.

On the way home, Pete and
Bob stop at Trey's house.
The hot chocolate is yummy.

"What a fun day!" says Pete.
"Tomorrow at school,
I'll tell my class all about it."

Pete wakes up to more snow.

It's not a school day.

It's another snow day!

Pete makes a snow fort.

He throws
snowballs.

He makes
a snow dog.

Then he has fun sledding.
He can't wait to tell
his teacher about it.

But the next day
is a snow day, too.

There's too
much snow!

Pete and Bob can barely even
open the front door.
"Before you go sledding,
please shovel the walk,"
says Mom.

But shoveling is hard work.
When Pete is done,
he's too tired to go sledding.

Pete misses his teacher.
He misses the other cats
in his class.

Pete can't wait to go back
to school tomorrow.

But when Pete wakes up,
it's snowing.
"Oh no!" he says.
"Not another snow day!"

Pete wants to go to school.
So Pete plows the streets
all by himself.

The other cats rush outside.

They help clear the snow.

Everyone wants to go to school.

The streets are clear and safe.

The bus can drive.

School is open!

All the kids are excited
to see their teacher.
He has a snow day
show-and-tell.

When it's Pete's turn,
he tells everyone about
the fun he had in the snow.

"I love snow days,"
says Pete.
"But I love school best!"

Pete the Cat
AND THE TIP-TOP TREE HOUSE

Pete the Cat has built a
tree house.

He calls his friends.

"I just built a tree house,"

he says.

"Come over to play."

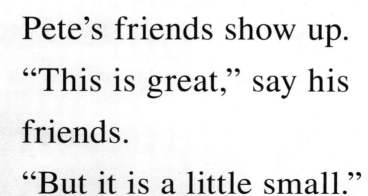

Pete's friends show up.
"This is great," say his
friends.
"But it is a little small."

"You are right," says Pete.
"It is too small.
I will fix that!"

Pete starts building a bigger
tree house.

"Do you want some help?"
asks Callie.

"Sure," says Pete.

Callie carries up more wood.

"Can I help, too?"
asks Marty.
"Sure!" says Pete.

Together they build a tower
for Pete's tree house.

"Let's have a tree house party," says Marty.

"A party?" says Pete.

"But what will everyone do?"

"I can help with that,"
says Emma.

"This is great!" says Pete.

"Let's do it."

Pete, Marty, Callie, Emma,
and Grumpy Toad get right
to work.

They build an arcade.

They fill it with fun games.

They build a bowling alley.

It has twenty lanes.

They build a wave pool.

Pete can surf indoors!

They build a movie theater

and a skate park

and a climbing wall

and an ice rink.

Pete's friends all come
for the party.

Pete takes one friend
to the bowling alley.

He takes one friend
to the movie theater.

Pete takes one friend
to the skate park.

Pete lets one friend surf
in the wave pool.

"Is everyone here?"
asks Pete.

"Yeah, but we're all alone!"
his friends say.
"We came to play with
each other."

"Oh!" says Pete.
"Everyone meet down
at the jungle gym."

Everyone climbs down.
"This tree house is
amazing," say his friends.

"Thanks,"
says Pete.

"I'm so glad it brought us
all together."

Pete the Cat
AND THE LOST TOOTH

Pete lost a tooth!
"Put it under your pillow,"
his mom says.
"The Tooth Fairy will come."

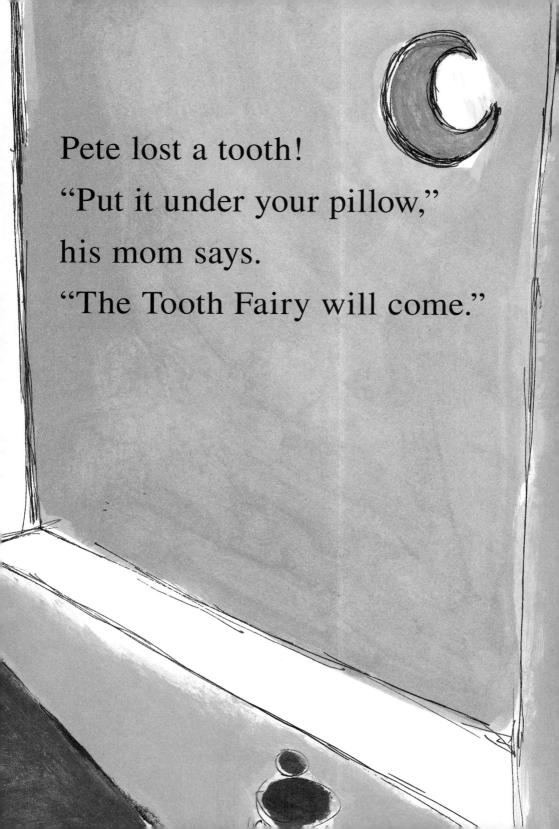

Pete puts the tooth
under his pillow.
He closes his eyes.

He hears a jingle.

It is the Tooth Fairy!

"I am very busy tonight,"
she says.
"I can help!" says Pete.

"Great!"
She gives Pete magic wings.
He can fly!

"Visit these cool kids,"
says the Tooth Fairy.

1. Callie
2. Alligator
3. Gus

"Just take the tooth and leave
a coin," she says.
Pete is ready to go!

Callie is first on the list.

There is Callie's lost tooth!

Pete takes the tooth.

He leaves a coin for Callie.

Alligator is next
on the list.

Look!

Alligator's lost tooth!

Careful! It is very sharp.

Pete takes the tooth.

He leaves a coin

for Alligator.

Gus the Platypus is
next on the list.

Uh-oh!

Where is the tooth?

The tooth is not here.

The tooth is not there.

The tooth is not anywhere!

Where is Gus's lost tooth?

The lost tooth is lost!

Does Pete panic?

Nope! He knows what to do.

Look! Gus is awake.

"Where is your tooth, Gus?"

Pete asks.

"Platypuses do not have teeth,"
says Gus.

"But I still want to be a part
of the Tooth Fairy fun!"

"No worries!" says Pete.
Pete puts a coin
under Gus's pillow.

147

"Thank you!" Gus says.

"You're welcome," says Pete.

"Good night, Gus!"

"Great work, Pete!" says
the Tooth Fairy.

"No problem!" says Pete.

Not everyone is the same.
But being kind is always cool.

Pete the Cat's

GROOVY

BAKE SALE

Pete the Cat is excited about his school bake sale.

Pete wants to bake a treat.

What should Pete bake?

Pete loves sweets.

Pete loves cookies.
Pete loves pies.

Pete loves brownies, cakes,
marshmallow treats,
and ice-cream sundaes.

"I'll make cookies!"
Pete thinks.

Pete takes out eggs,
flour, sugar, and of course,
chocolate chips.

He puts everything in a bowl.

He stirs and stirs.

Pete makes a big mess!

He rolls the dough into balls,
and his mom helps put them
into the oven.

They wait for the cookies
to bake.
They smell so yummy.

Then things smell less yummy.
Some of the cookies
are burned!

Pete has to start over.
What else can he make?

He tries to make
ice-cream sundaes,
but they turn into
ice-cream soup.

He tries to make
pudding pie
but runs out of crust.

The kitchen is a big mess.
He has no treats
for the bake sale.

"You'll find something yummy
to bring to the bake sale,"
says Pete's mom.

He has some berries,
vanilla pudding,
and a few cookie pieces.

"I've got it!" Pete says.
"I'll use a little bit
of all of it!"

So he adds whipped cream and
berries to the pudding and stirs.

Then he adds some cookie
pieces to the mix.

Carefully, he scoops some
onto a tray.

Pete puts the tray in the fridge.

The next morning,
it is a tray of tasty, groovy
berry goodness!

His mom helps him
scoop his treats into little cups.
He brings them to school.

Pete puts his berry cups
on the bake sale table.

"What is that?" asks Callie.
"Groovy berry goodness!"
says Pete.

His friends give it a try.

His dessert is a hit!

Soon all the treats are gone.

But Pete saves one.

He gives it to his mom.

"Thanks for your help!"

Groovy job!
Now you're moving on to

LEVEL ONE.

Pete the Cat

GOES CAMPING

Pete is excited to go camping!

This is his first time.

"Don't forget your sleeping bag!"

says Dad.

"Or your hiking boots!" Mom says.

The campsite is deep in the woods.

Mom and Dad set up the tent.

Pete and Bob help collect sticks
so they can make a fire later.

Pete and Bob go for a hike.

Bob shows Pete the footprints

of different animals.

"Do you think

we will see anything cool?"

asks Pete.

"Maybe," says Bob.

Pete and his dad go fishing.

They must be very quiet

and very still to catch a fish.

Fishing takes a long time.

They finally catch some fish.

Mom builds a fire.

She cooks the fish for dinner.

It tastes yummy.

Next Pete toasts marshmallows.
Pete makes s'mores with
chocolate and graham crackers.

It starts to get dark out.

Bob tells Pete a story

about a scary, hairy giant.

The giant lives in the woods.

His name is Bigfoot.

"Do you think Bigfoot lives *here*?"
asks Pete.

"No one has ever seen Bigfoot,"
says Bob.

"Don't let Bob scare you," says Dad.

"Bigfoot is not real," Mom says.

Pete sighs with relief!

"But if he is real, I bet he's friendly,"
says Dad, "and likes s'mores too!"

That's not scary, thinks Pete.

Maybe he wants a s'more.

Pete leaves one for his hairy friend.

Soon it's time for bed.

"Lights out, boys!" Dad says.

Bob and Pete share a tent.

Pete gets into his sleeping bag.

It is cozy, but he cannot sleep.

The woods seem extra dark.

And all the sounds

seem extra loud at night.

Pete hears a weird swooshing sound.

"What is that?" he asks Bob.

"That's just the wind," says Bob.

Pete hears an odd chirping noise.

"What is that?" he asks out loud.

Those are just the crickets.

Pete hears a strange hooting sound.

"What is that?" he wonders.

That's just an owl.

Pete thinks of his friend Owl.

Pete hears a loud snapping sound.

CRACK!

"What is that?" he wonders.

But Bob is already fast asleep.

Pete listens carefully.

CRACK!

Is it Bigfoot?

Pete peeks outside.

It is too dark to see anything.

When Pete wakes up, he checks

the spot where he left

the s'more for Bigfoot.

The s'more is gone!

There is a note.

It says, "Thanks for the

treat! XOXO"

Pete shows his family.

"Wow, I knew Bigfoot was real!"

says Bob.

Pete knows Bigfoot is not scary.

Just because he looks different

does not mean he is scary.

He even likes s'mores too!

Pete the Cat

AND THE COOL CATERPILLAR

Pete is on a bug safari!

He and his friends
are looking for bugs.
How many bugs can they find?

Callie spots a tiny black ant.

"It's building an anthill!" she says.

"Groovy!" says Pete.

Gus finds a round red ladybug in the mint patch.

"It has nine spots!" says Gus.

"Nice!" says Pete.

Marty sees a big black spider.

"It caught a fly," he says.

"Neat," says Pete.

Pete finds a green caterpillar
in the flowerpot.
"I will bring it home to show
Mom and Dad," he says.

Mom helps Pete build a home for
the caterpillar.

They use a big jar.

Dad puts lots of little holes in
the lid for air.

Pete puts the caterpillar
in the jar.

Pete puts some leaves in the jar

for the caterpillar to eat.

He adds a twig for it to crawl on.

"Good night, Pete," says Mom.

"Good night, Pete," says Dad.

"Good night, caterpillar,"
says Pete.

When Pete wakes up,

the caterpillar is gone!

Where did it go?

Did it run away?

"It is not gone," says Mom.

"It did not run away," says Dad.

"Look!" they say.

"The caterpillar is inside there,"

says Mom.

"It's called a pupa."

"Will it stay in there forever?"

Pete asks.

"No," says Dad. "The caterpillar is changing into something new."

"What will it become?" Pete asks.

"It's a surprise," says Mom.

"We must wait and see."

Pete waits.

Callie comes to visit.

"Did it come out yet?" she asks.

"Not yet," says Pete.

Pete waits some more.

Gus comes to visit.

"Did it come out yet?" he asks.

"Not yet," says Pete.

Pete waits even longer.

Marty comes to visit.

"Did it come out yet?" he asks.

"Not yet," says Pete.

Pete waits

and waits

and waits.

234

Then, one day,

something finally happens.

The pupa starts to wiggle!

"Something is happening!" says Pete.

It wiggles some more.

Everyone comes over to watch.

The pupa cracks open.

Something is coming out!

What can it be?

A head pokes out,

then some legs,

and then two colorful wings.

The caterpillar changed into

a beautiful butterfly!

"Wow!" says Pete.

The butterfly slowly moves
its wings up and down.
It is ready to fly.

They take the jar to the park.

"Time to say goodbye," says Dad.

Pete opens the lid of the jar.

The butterfly flaps its wings.
It flutters out of the jar and
lands on Pete's nose.
"That tickles!" he says.

Then the butterfly flies up into
the sky.

"Bye-bye, butterfly!" everyone says.

"Let's find a new caterpillar!"

says Pete.

"Change is pretty cool!"

Pete the Cat's

FUNKY FAMILY TREE

Pete is making a family tree.

A family tree is a drawing.

A family tree shows

all the people in your family.

Mom and Dad are helping Pete
make his family tree.

First Pete adds Mom, Dad,

and Bob to the family tree.

"Now what?" Pete asks.

"Now we add your grandparents,"
says Mom.

Mom's mom is Pete's Grandma Greta.

Grandma Greta is a boat captain.

She sails all over the world.

Pete makes believe

that he is sailing on a ship.

"Ahoy!" says Pete.

Mom's dad is Pete's Grandpa Bubba.

Grandpa Bubba is a baseball player.

"Hey! I love playing baseball too!"
says Pete.

Pete swings a make-believe bat.

Dad's mom is Pete's Nana Thelma.

Nana Thelma works in a library.

She loves to read books.

"Cool!" says Pete.

Pete also loves to read books.

Dad's dad is Pete's Pop-Pop Scott.

Pop-Pop Scott is a baker.

He bakes yummy cupcakes and cookies.

POP-POP SCOTT

"I love cupcakes!" says Pete.

"Oh, and cookies too!"

"Is that it?" Pete asks.

"No. There's more," says Dad.

"Our family is big," says Mom.

"They came from around the world,"
says Dad.

Pete draws more branches on
his family tree.

One of Pete's great-grandfathers
worked in a castle, long ago.
He kept the king safe!

GREAT-GRANDFATHER

OSCAR

Pete imagines that he is a royal guard!

"Halt!" Pete shouts.

One of Pete's great-grandmothers
was a great magician.
She knew many cool magic tricks.

GREAT - GRANDMOTHER

HILDA

Pete puts on his magic hat.

"Abracadabra!" says Pete.

"Did you tell Pete about Pete yet?"

Mom asks.

"I'm Pete," says Pete.

"But long ago,

there was another Pete," says Dad.

"We named you after him," says Mom.

"What was he like?" asks Pete.

GREAT-UNCLE PETE

"Great-Uncle Pete played music
in a band," says Mom.

"Everyone loved his music," Dad says.

"I like to play music too!" says Pete.

"What else did Great-Uncle Pete do?"

"Great-Uncle Pete painted pretty art,"
says Mom.
Mom shows Pete pictures
of Great-Uncle Pete's art.

"I like to paint too!" says Pete.

"Tell me more about Great-Uncle Pete."

"Great-Uncle Pete loved to surf,"
says Dad.
"He even won a prize for surfing!"
says Mom.

"Maybe I can win a surfing prize!"
says Pete.

He pretends to surf a big wave.

"Pete is a good name for me,"
says Pete.

"It is," says Dad.

"But you are *you*!" Mom says.

"Why?" asks Pete.

"Because you are *our* Pete,"

says Mom.

"We love you most of all,"

says Dad.

Pete's family is full of cool people.

His family has many cool stories.

Pete loves his family, and he loves

Mom, Dad, and Bob most of all.

CONGRATULATIONS!

You're one cool reader.
You read nine I Can Reads
with **Pete** the **Cat!**